Albert's Bri

C000294351

A play

Tom Stoppard

Samuel French - London
New York - Toronto - Hollywood

CHARACTERS

Bob
Charlie
Dad
Albert
The Chairman
Dave
George
Fitch
Albert's Mother
Kate
Albert's Father
Fraser
Voices in the Darkness

*The action of the play takes place on a bridge, in offices,
a boardroom, the Eiffel Tower, a bedroom, and two
living-rooms*

AUTHOR'S NOTE

Albert's Bridge was written for radio, and little or no attempt has been made to adapt the script for the stage; this edition, therefore, might be described as a director's challenge. A very free approach to the printed stage directions, seems to me to be warranted, particularly to avoid pauses between scenes and to keep the thing flowing. To take one example, it may not be necessary to furnish Fitch's office with a desk and chairs; a couple of "spots" on the faces might be enough, for the conversation does not *have* to take place in an office. Alternatively, where back projection is available, a slide of a filing cabinet and a wall-chart is enough to say "office" to the audience. Furthermore, again in the interests of flow, I doubt that, for example, the "bridge area" and the "home area" need be considered as rigidly separate worlds: Albert on the bridge could talk to Kate at home. Feel free.

T. S.

ALBERT'S BRIDGE

SCENE 1

Part of a big girdered railway bridge.

Four men are painting the bridge, in ascending order: Bob, Charlie, Dad, Albert.

Bob Char-lee!
Charlie Hel-lo!
Bob Right, Charlie?
Charlie Right! Comin' down! Hey, Dad!
Dad Hel-lo!
Charlie Bob 'n me is done down here!
Dad Right!
Charlie Have you done?
Dad Comin' down! Albert! Al-bert!
Charlie Albert!
Bob Al-bert!
Albert (*crooning softly, tunelessly amid various tunes while painting*)
How high the moon in June?
How blue the moon when it's high noón—
and the turtle doves above
croon out of tune in love
saying please above the trees
which when there's thunder you don't run under—
those trees—
'cos there'll be pennies fall on Alabama
and you'll drown in foggy London town
the sun was shining—on my Yiddisher Mama.
Bob Albert!
Charlie Albert!
Dad Albert!
Albert Hel-lo!
Dad Bob 'n me 'n Charlie's done!

Albert Right! Dip-brush-slap-slide-slick, and once again, dip, brush, slap—oh, it goes on so nicely. Tickle it into the corner, there, behind the rivet. No-one will see that from the ground; I could cheat up here. But I'd know; so dip, brush, slap, slide and once again for the last time till the next time—every sur-face sleek, renewed—dip, brush, slap, slick, tickle and wipe—right in there with the old rust-proof, rust-brown—all glossed and even, end to end—the last touch—perfection!

He stops painting

Oh my! I could stand back to admire it and fall three hundred feet into the sea. Mind your heads! (*He laughs. Climbing down*) Mind your head, Dad!

Dad I'm not your dad. Keep off the wet—work down the slope to the middle—and watch your feet.

They all slowly start climbing down

Going down for good, oh, yes, I'm not facing that again. Ten coats I've done, end to end and now I'm done all right. I had ambitions, you know . . .

Charlie Mind my head, Dad.

Dad Watch my feet, Charlie—comin' down . . .

Charlie I'll watch your feet—you mind my head. Watch your head, Bob . . .

Bob Watch your feet, Charlie . . .

Charlie Mind my feet, Bob—watch my head, Dad . . .

Dad I'm not your dad, and mind my feet—that's my head, Albert.

Albert Comin' down. Doesn't she look beautiful?

Dad Looks the same as always. There's no progress. Twenty years, twenty thousand pots of paint—yes, I had plans.

Charlie. I thought we'd never see the end of it.

Bob It's not the bleeding end.

Charlie There's no end to it.

Dad Ten coats non-stop, one after the other, and it's no improve-ment, no change even, just holding its own against the weather —that's a long time, that's a lot of paint. I could have made my mark.

Albert Continuity—that's hard to come by.

Dad I've spread my life over those girders, and in five minutes

I could scrape down to the iron, I could scratch down to my prime.

Albert Simplicity—so . . . contained; neat; your bargain with the world, your wages, your time, your energy, your property, everything you took out and everything you put in, the bargain that has carried you this far—all contained there in ten layers of paint, accounted for; now that's something; to keep track of everything you put into the kitty, to have it lie there, under your eye, fixed and immediate—there are no consequences to a coat of paint. That's more than you can say for a factory man; his bits and pieces scatter, grow wheels, disintegrate, change colour, join up in new forms which he doesn't know anything about; in short he doesn't know what he's done to whom.

Dad Watch your feet, Albert. Mind your head, Charlie.

Charlie You mind my head. Take care my feet, Bob . . .

Bob Watch your feet, Charlie . . .

Charlie Mind your feet, Dad . . .

Dad That's my head, Albert . . .

Albert Coming down . . . Ah, look at it up there, criss-crossed and infinite, you can't see where it ends—I could take off and swing through its branches screaming like a gibbon!

Dad Mind where you're putting your feet, Albert.

Charlie Watch my head, Dad.

Bob Train coming, Charlie.

A distant train is heard approaching

Charlie I've seen it.

Bob (*jumping down on to the gravel*) And down.

Charlie Mind where you jump, Dad.

Dad Seen it.

Charlie (*jumping down*) None too soon.

Dad Train coming, Albert.

Albert I'm with you.

Dad (*jumps down*) Finished.

Charlie Like hell.

Bob Well, that's another two years behind you.

Dad A feller once offered me a half share in a very nice trading station in the China Seas. I had it in me.

Albert Mind your toes. (*He jumps down*) Now that's a good way to end a day—ending so much else.

Charlie All right for some. Students.

Bob Slummers.

Charlie Pocket-money holiday lads, oh yes.

Albert One bridge, freshly painted—a million tons of iron thrown across the bay—rust brown and even to the last lick —spick and span, rust-proofed, weather resistant—perfect!

Dad Other end needs painting now. A man could go mad.

The train passes overhead

The scene closes

SCENE 2

A committee-room.

The Chairman, George, Dave and Fitch are seated round the table. Fitch wears rimless spectacles and is confident in manner, with a clipped, distinctive voice.

The Chairman Let us not forget, gentlemen, that Clufton Bay Bridge is the fourth biggest single-span double-track shore-to-shore railway bridge in the world bar none.

Dave Hear, hear, Mr Chairman.

The Chairman Thank you, Dave.

George I've been studying these figures, Mr Chairman . . .

The Chairman Just a moment, George. We've got an amenity here in Clufton, that bridge stands for the whole town, quite apart from the money earned in railway dues . . .

Dave Hear, hear, Mr Chairman.

The Chairman Thank you, Dave.

George According to the City Engineer's figures, Mr Chairman . . .

The Chairman Just a moment, George. When my grandfather built this bridge he didn't spare the brass—and I for one, as Chairman of the Clufton Bay Bridge Sub-Committee—entrusted as we are with the upkeep and responsibility of what is a symbol of Clufton's prosperity—I for one do not begrudge the spending of a few extra quid on a lick of paint.

Dave Hear, hear, Mr Chairman.

The Chairman Thank you, Dave.

George I know it's a symbol of your prosperity, Mr Chairman, but . . .

The Chairman That's a highly improper remark, George. Clufton's prosperity is what I said.

Dave Hear hear, Mr Chairman.

The Chairman Thank you, Dave.

George My mistake, Mr Chairman—but if Mr Fitch's figures are correct . . .

Fitch My figures are always correct, Mr Chairman.

The Chairman Hear that, George? The City Engineer's figures are a model of correctitude.

Dave Hear hear, Mr Chairman.

The Chairman Thank you, Dave.

George Then this new paint he's recommending is going to cost us four times as much as the paint we've been using up to now.

The Chairman (*after a pause*) Four times as much? Money?

Dave Hear hear, Mr Chairman.

The Chairman Just a moment, Dave. I don't think your figures are correct, George. Mr Fitch knows his business.

George What business is he in—paint?

The Chairman That's a highly improper remark, George—er, you're not in the paint business, are you, Mr Fitch?

Fitch No, Mr Chairman.

The Chairman No, no, of course you're not. You should be ashamed, George.

Dave Hear hear, Mr Chairman.

The Chairman Shut up, Dave. Now what about it, Mr Fitch—is this right what George says?

Fitch Well, up to a point, Mr Chairman, yes. But in the long run, no.

The Chairman Don't fiddle-faddle with me, Fitch. Does this new-fangled paint of yours cost four times as much as the paint we've got, and if so what's in it for you?

George Hear hear, Mr Chairman.

The Chairman Thank you, George.

Fitch To put the matter at its simplest, Mr Chairman, the new paint costs four times as much and last four times as long.

The Chairman Well, there's your answer, George. It costs four times as much but it lasts four times as long. Very neat, Fitch.

George What's the point, then?

Fitch Apart from its silvery colour, Mr Chairman, which would be a pleasanter effect than the present rusty brown, the new paint would also afford a considerable saving, as you can no doubt see.

The Chairman Everybody see that? Well, I don't.

George Nor do I.

Dave Hear hear, George.

George Shut up, Dave.

Fitch If I might explain, gentlemen. As you know, in common with other great bridges of its kind, the painting of Clufton Bay Bridge is a continuous operation. That is to say, by the time the painters have reached the far end, the end they started at needs painting again.

Dave I never knew that!

The Chairman }
George } *(speaking together)* Shut up, Dave.

Fitch This cycle is not a fortuitous one. It is contrived by relating the area of the surfaces to be painted—call it A—to the rate of the painting—B—and the durability of the paint—C. The resultant equation determines the variable factor X—i.e. the number of painters required to paint surfaces A at speed B within time C. For example . . .

The Chairman E.g.

Fitch Quite. Er, e.g., with X plus one painters the work would proceed at a higher rate—i.e. B plus, e.g. Q. However, the factors A and C, the surface area and the lasting quality of the paint remain, of course, constant. The result would be that the painters would be ready to begin painting the bridge for the second time strictly speaking before it needed re-painting. This creates the coefficient—Waste.

The Chairman W.

Fitch If you like. This coefficient belies efficiency you see.

The Chairman *(indulging in schoolboy humour with George)* U.C. You see, George?

George O.K., I see.

Fitch To continue. Furthermore, the value of the coefficient—Waste—is progressive. Let me put it like this, gentlemen. Because the rate of painting is constant, i.e. too fast to allow the paintwork to deteriorate, each bit the men come to requires re-painting even less than the bit before it. You see, they are all the time catching up on themselves progressively, until there'll come a point where they'll be re-painting the bridge while it's still wet! (*He pauses*) No, that can't be right . . .

The Chairman Come to the point, Fitch. Wake up, Dave.

Dave (*waking up*) Hear hear, Mr Chairman.

Fitch To put it another way, gentlemen, that is to say, conversely. With one too few painters—X minus one—the rate of progress goes down to, let us say, B minus Q. So what is the result? By the time the painters are ready to start re-painting, the end they started at has deteriorated into unsightly and damaging rust—a coefficient representing the converse inefficiency.

The Chairman Pull yourself together, Fitch—I don't know what you're drivellin' about.

George In a nutshell, Fitch—the new paint costs four times as much and last four times as long. Where's the money saved?

Fitch We sack three painters.

The Chairman (*after a pause*) Ah . . .

Fitch You see, to date we have achieved our optimum efficiency by employing four men. It takes them two years to paint the bridge, which is the length of time the paint lasts. This new paint will last eight years, so we only need one painter to paint the bridge by himself. After eight years, the end he started at will be just ready for re-painting. The saving to the rate-payers would be three thousand, five hundred and twenty-nine pounds fifteen shillings and ninepence per annum.

George Excuse me, Mr Chairman . . .

The Chairman Just a moment, George. I congratulate you, Mr Fitch. An inspired stroke. We'll put it up to a meeting of the full council.

George Excuse me . . .

The Chairman Shut up, George.

Dave Hear hear, Mr Chairman.

Fitch Thank you, Mr Chairman.

The Chairman Thank you, Mr Fitch.

The scene closes

SCENE 3

Albert's bedroom.

Albert is in bed. His mother stands by his side.

Mother Aren't you getting up, Albert? It's gone eleven. Are you listening to me, Albert?

Albert What?

Mother I'm talking to you, Albert.

Albert Yes?

Mother Yes—what?

Albert Yes, Mother.

Mother That's better. Oh dear, what was I saying?

Albert I don't know, Mother.

Mother (*sighing*) I was against that university from the start.

Albert The country needs universities.

Mother I mean it's changed you, Albert. You're thinking all the time. It's not like you, Albert.

Albert Thinking?

Mother You don't talk to me. Or your father. Well, I'm glad it's all behind you, I hope it starts to wear off.

Albert I wanted to stay on after my degree, but they wouldn't have me.

Mother I don't know what you want to know about philosophy for. Your father didn't have to study philosophy and look where he is—chairman of Metal Alloys and Allied Metals. It's not as if you were going to be a philosopher or something. Yes, you could have been a trainee executive by now. As it is you'll have to do your stint on the factory floor, philosophy or no philosophy. That university has held you back.

Albert I'll have to get myself articled to a philosopher. Start at the bottom. Of course, a philosopher's clerk wouldn't get the really interesting work straight off, I know that. It'll be a matter of filing the generalizations, tidying up the paradoxes, laying out the premises before the boss gets in—that kind of thing; but after I've learned the ropes I might get a half share in a dialectic, perhaps, and work up towards a treatise. Yes, I could have my own thriving little philosopher's office in a few years.

Mother (*after a pause*) Would you like to have some coffee downstairs?

Albert Yes.

Mother Yes what?

Albert Yes, please.

Mother (*after a pause*) I still think it was mean of you not to let us know you had a summer vacation.

Albert I thought you knew. I've had one every year.

Mother You know I've no head for dates. You could have come home to see us.

Albert I'm sorry—there was this temporary job going . . .

Mother Your father would have given you some money if you'd asked him.

Albert I thought I'd have a go myself.

Mother You'll have to get up now.

Albert It was fantastic up there. The scale of it. From the ground it looks just like a cat's cradle, from a distance you can take it all in, and then up there in the middle of it the thinnest threads are as thick as your body and you could play tennis on the main girders . . .

Mother Kate will be up in a minute to make the beds.

Albert It's absurd, really, being up there, looking down on the university lying under you like a couple of bricks, full of dots studying philosophy . . .

Mother I don't want you getting in Kate's way—she's got to clean.

Albert What could they possibly know? I saw more up there in three weeks than those dots in three years. I saw the context. It reduced philosophy and everything else. I got a perspective. Because that bridge was—separate—complete—removed, defined by principles of engineering which makes it stop at a certain point, which compels a certain shape, certain joints——the whole thing utterly fixed by the rules that make it stay up. It's complete, and a man can give his life to its maintenance, a very fine bargain.

Mother Do you love me, Albert?

Albert Yes.

Mother Yes what?

Albert Yes, please.

The lights fade. A gavel is heard banging on a table

Mayoral Voice (*in the darkness*) Number forty-three on the order paper, proposal from Bridge Sub-committee . . .
First Voice (*in the darkness*) Move . . .
Second Voice (*in the darkness*) Second.
Mayoral Voice (*in the darkness*) All in favour . . .

An absent-minded murmur of fifty "Ayes" is heard

Against (*Pause*) Carried. Number forty-four on the order paper . . .

The lights come up on Albert's bedroom. There is a knock on the door, which is opened

Kate (*off*) Oh, I'm sorry, Mr Albert.
Albert Hello, I was just thinking of getting up.

The scene closes

SCENE 4

Fitch's office.

Fitch is at his desk, talking to Bob.

Bob What—by myself? It would take years.
Fitch Eight years, yes.
Bob No. I demand a transfer.
Fitch I thought I'd give you first refusal.
Bob I want to go back to painting the Corporation crest on the dustcarts.
Fitch I could fit you in on the magenta.
Bob On the what?
Fitch It's one man to a colour nowadays. Efficiency.

The lights fade, then come up again on Fitch and Charlie

Charlie You must be joking.
Fitch It's an opportunity for you.
Charlie I'd go mad. What's it all about?

Fitch Efficiency.

Charlie I'm not doing that bridge on me tod.

Fitch It's no more work than before.

Charlie I'd jump off within a month.

Fitch Oh. Well, we couldn't have that. That would be only one-ninety-sixth of it done.

The lights fade, then come up again on Fitch and Dad

Dad You mean it's a cheaper way of doing it.

Fitch More efficient.

Dad We've been doing a good job.

Fitch Efficiency isn't a matter of good and bad, entirely. It's a matter of optimum use of resources—time, money, manpower.

Dad You mean it's cheaper. I'm an old man.

Fitch You've got eight years in you.

Dad It might be my last eight. I haven't done anything yet—I've got a future.

Fitch Well, I could put you on yellow no-parking lines.

Dad Yes, all right.

The lights fade, then come up again on Fitch and Albert

Fitch But do you have any qualifications?

Albert I've got a degree in philosophy, Mr Fitch.

Fitch That's a little unusual.

Albert I wouldn't say that. There were lots of us doing it.

Fitch That's all very well if you're going to be a philosopher, but what we're talking about is painting bridges.

Albert Yes, yes, I can see what you're driving at, of course, but I don't suppose it did me any harm. Almost everyone who didn't know what to do, did philosophy. Well, that's logical.

Fitch You're an educated man.

Albert Thank you.

Fitch What I mean, you're not the run of the mill bridge painter, not the raw material I'm looking for.

Albert Well, I did it in the vacation.

Fitch Yes—yes, I did have reports of you. But surely . . .

Albert I know what you mean, but that's what I want to do. I liked it. I don't want to work in a factory or an office.

Fitch Is it the open-air life that attracts you?

Albert No. It's the work, the whole thing—crawling round that great basket, so high up, being responsible for so much that's visible. Actually I don't know if that's why I like it. I like it because I was happy up there, doing something simple but so grand, without end. It doesn't get away from you.

Fitch The intellectual rather than the practical—that's it, is it?

Albert Probably.

Fitch I'm the same. It's poetry to me—a perfect equation of space, time and energy . . .

Albert Yes . . .

Fitch It's not just slapping paint on a girder . . .

Albert No . . .

Fitch It's continuity, control—mathematics.

Albert Poetry.

Fitch Yes, I should have known it was a job for a university man.

Albert Like me and you . . .

Fitch Well, I went to night school myself.

Albert Same thing, different time.

Fitch That's what I say.

Albert I'm your man, Mr Fitch.

Fitch You'll stick to it for eight years, will you?

Albert Oh, I'll paint it more than once.

The scene closes

SCENE 5

Living-room at Albert's home.

Albert, Father and Mother are seated at breakfast.

Father Now then, Albert, you've had your fun. When I was your age I'd got six years of work behind me.

Albert Well, I'm starting work now, Father.

Father Quite so, but don't think you're going to start at the top. You'll get there all right in time, but you've got to learn the business first. Is there any more tea, Mother?

Mother Ring for Kate, would you, Albert?

Albert Yes, Mother. (*He rings the bell*)

Mother That reminds me . . .

Father You'll start where I started. On the shop floor.

Albert Well, actually father . . .

Mother I don't want to sound Victorian, but one can't just turn a blind eye.

Albert What?

Father Yes, I never went in for books and philosophy and look at me now.

Mother I suppose that's the penance one pays for having servants nowadays.

Albert What?

Father I started Metal Alloys and Allied Metals—built it up from a small biscuit-tin furnace in the back garden, small smelting jobs for the cycle-repair shop.

Mother I've suspected her for some time and now one can't ignore it. Even with her corset.

Albert Who?

Father You can come in on Monday and I'll hand you over to the plant foreman.

Albert I've already got a job. Actually.

Father You haven't got a job until I give you one.

Albert I'm going to paint Clufton Bay Bridge, starting Monday.

Mother What colour?

Albert Silver.

Father Just a minute . . .

Kate enters

Kate You rang, madam?

Mother More tea, Kate, please.

Kate Yes, madam.

Mother And a word.

Kate Yes, madam.

Mother Are you ill?

Kate No, madam.

Mother I believe I heard you being ill in the bathroom this morning.

Kate Yes, madam.

Mother And yesterday?

Kate Yes, madam.

Albert What's the matter, Kate?

Kate Nothing, Mr Albert.

Mother Leave this to me. Cook tells me you fainted in the kitchen last week.

Kate I came over funny.

Albert Kate . . .

Mother Let's not beat about the bush. Is it the gardener's boy?

Kate No, madam.

Mother Then who is it?

Albert Who's what?

Mother Well, I'm sorry. You can have a month's wages, of course. You'd better make sure that the young man does the right thing by you.

The lights fade. A wedding march is heard—but a "Muzale" version suitable for a civil wedding; not a church organ. The lights come up again to reveal Kate and Albert alone together

Kate I never thought you'd do the right thing by me, Albert.

Albert We'll be all right. It's a nice room.

Kate Your mum didn't like it.

Albert My mother's got no taste. I'll make a fire.

Kate And wrap up warm when you go out—it'll be freezing up there.

Albert Only a breeze.

Kate It'll be ice in a month. If you fell I'd die, Albert.

Albert So would I.

Kate Don't you ever fall. They shouldn't make it a year-round job. It's dangerous.

Albert No—you don't know how big it is—the threads are like ladders and the cross-pieces are like piers into the sky.

Kate You hold on tight, for the spring, and the baby.

The scene closes

SCENE 6

The bridge.

Albert is at work painting.

Albert
  Slip, slap, brush, dip, slop, slide,
  slick and wipe. In eight years I'll be
  pushing thirty, and the Clufton Bay Bridge will be
  a silver bridge—dip-brush, slick, slide, slap without
  end, I'm the bridge man, web-spinning silvering spiderman
  crawling between heaven and earth on a cantilevered
  span,
  cat's cradled in the sky . . .
  look down look down at the toy ships
  where the sea pounds under toy trains to toy
  towns
  under my hand.
  Am I the spider or the fly?
  I'm the bridge man . . .

  The downstairs maid went upstairs to make
  a bed that I was in—and suddenly . . .

A baby cries

The scene closes

SCENE 7

Albert's and Kate's home.

Albert and Kate are standing with the baby.

Albert I name this child Albert.
Kate You can't.
Albert Very well. I name this child Kate.
Kate Katherine.
Albert Tomorrow wheel her along to the bridge so I can see
  you.

Kate All right. But don't wave, Albert. Don't wave. If you waved
    and fell . . .
Albert I shan't wave.

                        The scene closes

                        SCENE 8
The bridge.

Albert is discovered painting.

Albert
    Dip brush, dip brush
    without end, come rain or shine;
    A fine way to spend my time.
    My life is set out for me,
    the future traced in brown,
    my past measured in silver;
    how absurd, how sublime
    (don't look down)
    to climb and clamber in a giant frame;
    dip brush, dip brush, click, slide wipe
    and again.

He stops painting

    I straddle a sort of overflowing gutter on
    which bathtub boats push up and down. The
    banks are littered with various bricks,
    kiddiblocks with windows; dinky toys move
    through the gaps, dodged by moving dots that
    have no colour; under my feet the triang train
    thunders across the meccano, and the minibrick
    estates straggle up over the hill in neat
    rows with paintbox gardens. It's the most
    expensive toytown in the store—the detail
    is remarkable. But fragile. I tremble for it,
    half expecting some petulant pampered child
    to step over the hill and kick the whole thing
    to bits.

He paints

Don't look down,
the dots are looking up.
Don't wave, don't fall, tumbling down a
telescope, diminishing to a dot.
In eight years who will I be?
Not me.
I'll be assimilated then,
the honest working man, father of three—
you've seen him around,
content in his obscurity, come to terms with public truths,
digging the garden of a council house
in what is now my Sunday suit.
I'm okay for fifty years, with any luck;
I can see me climb
up a silver bridge to paint it for the seventh time,
keeping track of my life spent in painting in the colour of my
    track:
above it all.
How sublime
(dip brush, dip brush) silvering the brown.
Which dot is mine?
Don't wave, don't look down.
Don't fall.

The scene close

SCENE 9

Albert's home

Albert and Kate are sitting together.

Kate I saw you today.
Albert What was I doing?
Kate Painting, I suppose. Crawling along a cross-piece.
Albert Pulling silver after me. I didn't see you. Or I didn't see
    which one was you.
Kate Coming out of the hairdressers. Six-and-six, I had it cut.

Albert Just goes to show—if you get far enough away, six and sixpence doesn't show, and nor does anything, at a distance.

Kate Well, life is all close up, isn't it?

Albert Yes, it hits you, when you come back down. How close it all is. You can't stand back to look at it.

Kate Do you like my hair like this?

Albert Like what? Oh—yes. Do you like mine?

Kate I got whistled at in the street.

Albert It's always happening to me.

Kate A lorry driver, at the traffic lights.

Albert They're worst, I find.

Kate Oh, Albert. I had the pram with me too.

Albert You look too young for it. Big sister.

Kate And I cook very nice, don't I?

Albert I'd whistle at you.

Kate I'd come, if you whistled. I'd give you a wink and say, "Cheeky!"

Albert Oh, yes—you'd get off with me. No trouble at all. I'd take you down by the canal after the pictures.

Kate What do you know about it?—with your education and all.

Albert Me? I'm a working man.

Kate You don't have regrets, do you, Albert?

Albert No.

Kate It wasn't a good bargain, on the face of it.

Albert It depends what you want.

Kate Me and the baby. Two rooms and a forty-five-hour week, hard work, and no advancement.

Albert I'm not ambitious.

Kate You could have had so much—a white wedding, nice house, an office job with real prospects, the country club—tennis. Yes, you could have had Metal Alloys and Allied Metals—the top job, responsibility, your own office with telephones . . .

Albert Yes, I'm well out of that.

The scene closes

SCENE 10

The Bridge.

Albert is discovered painting.

Albert
Progress. Two lines of silver meeting up in an
angle bracket—and tickle in there behind the rivet—
slip slop and wipe and on we go up the slope.

Does the town look up? Do they all gawp and say to
each other "Look at him! How ridiculous he looks up
there, so small, how laughably inadequate." Or do they
say, "How brave! One man against the elements!
Pitted against so much! The lone explorer feeling his
way between the iron crevasses, tacked against the sky
by his boots and fingers."

Dots, bricks and beetles.
I could drown them in my spit.

The scene closes

SCENE 11

Albert's Home.

Albert, Kate and the baby are together.

Kate That isn't nice, Albert.
Albert Spitting?
Kate Talking like that.
Albert It doesn't represent desire. I'll let them live. I'm only
trying to tell you what it's like.
Kate I know what it's like. It's painting a girder. There's other
jobs.
Albert It's my bridge—I wish you'd stop her rattling, it's getting
on my nerves.
Kate That's very advanced for six months.

Albert I'm not doubting her progress. If she played the trumpet
it would be even more advanced but it would still be sending
me round the twist. Here, give . . .

He takes the rattle from the baby, who bawls

Kate Now you've set her off. She doesn't understand. (*Comfort-
ing*) Come on, then . . .
Albert Well, see you later.
Kate Where are you going?
Albert Work.
Kate It's your Saturday off.
Albert No, it's my Saturday on.
Kate Last Saturday was your Saturday on.
Albert Well, I'll take two off in a row.

The scene closes

SCENE 12

The bridge.

Albert is discovered painting.

Albert
    Listen—
    The hot sun makes you think of insects,
    but this insect hum is the whole city
    caught in a seashell . . .
    All conversation is hidden there,
    among motors, coughing fits, applause,
    screams, laughter, feet on the stairs,
    secretaries typing to dictation,
    radios delivering cricket scores,
    tape running, wheels turning, mills grinding,
    chips frying, lavatories flushing, lovers sighing,
    the mayor blowing his nose.
    All audible life in the vibration
    of a hairdryer in the room below.

He paints

Dip brush slide stroke,
it goes on as smooth and shiny
as my sweat. I itch.
Paint on my arm,
silver paint on my brown arm;
it could be part of the bridge.

He stops painting

Listen. The note of Clufton is B flat.
The whole world could be the same.
Look down. Is it a fact
that all the dots have names?

> *The scene closes*

SCENE 13

Albert's home.

Kate and Albert are talking together.

Kate Jack Morris is taking Maureen and little Leslie to Paris.
Albert Who's Jack Morris?
Kate Next door, Albert.
Albert Oh, yes. Who's Maureen?
Kate Mrs Morris.
Albert So little Leslie would be their little girl.
Kate It's a little boy.
Albert Ah. Why are we talking about them?
Kate They're going to Paris for a holiday. Where are we going?
Albert When?
Kate That's what I'd like to know.
Albert What?
Kate Don't you have a holiday?
Albert Oh. I suppose I must. Everybody does. Yes, I expect
    Fitch took that into account.
Kate You're not going to dodge your holiday—I know what
    you're up to, you're already working full Saturdays, don't

think I'm such a fool that I don't know. And you're working till dark.

Albert Overtime. I lose time in the winter.

Kate (*sniffing*) It's because you don't like it here, being at home.

Albert Oh, Kate—I've got a schedule, you see.

Kate You're miles ahead of it.

Albert I've got to have some in hand in case of accidents.

Kate I told you! You'll fall off, and me and Katherine will be alone. (*She cries*)

Albert No, no, no—stop crying. We'll have a holiday. I'll take a week.

Kate A fortnight.

Albert All right, I don't mind.

Kate Can we go to Paris?

Albert I've been to Paris. There's nothing there, believe me. We could go to Scotland.

Kate Touring.

Albert Certainly. The Firth of Forth.

Kate We haven't got a car. Maureen said we could go with them.

Albert But they're going to Paris.

Kate We could afford it. It wouldn't be hard, it's easier with two children and joined forces. It would be lovely, I've always wanted to see the Champs Elysee and the Arc de Triumph and the Seine and the Eiffel Tower . . .

The scene closes

SCENE 14

A section of the Eiffel Tower, looking the same as Clufton Bridge.

Cliché French accordion music is heard. Albert is seen on the Tower. Kate calls from below.

Kate (*off*) Albert! A-a-albert! Come down! Please come down . . .

Albert I thought as much. Dots, bricks, beetles—in B flat. Still, I'm glad I came. The pointlessness takes one's breath away— a tower connects nothing, it stands only so that one can go up and look down. Bridge-builders have none of this audacity, compromise themselves with function. Monsieur Eiffel, poet and philosopher, every eight years I'll scratch your name in the silver of Clufton Bay Bridge.

Kate (*in the distance: despairingly*) Al-bert!

Albert (*quietly*) Coming down.

The scene closes

SCENE 15

Albert's home.

Albert and Kate are discovered in the middle of a quarrel. Kate throws a cup at Albert.

Kate What's her name?

Albert Kate . . .

Kate What a bloody coincidence!

Albert You've got it all wrong, Kate, there's no woman . . .

Kate (*crying*) I can smell her on your coat?

Albert It's paint—I tell you I was up on the bridge.

Kate All night!

Albert I just thought I would. It was nice up there.

Kate You're barmy if you expect me to believe that, you're round the twist.

Albert It's true!

Kate And I believe it, I am round the twist! I'm as barmy as you are, but I believe it.

Albert That's better . . .

Kate throws another cup at Albert

Kate No, it isn't—it's worse! A woman would be normal. (*Breaking down*) You don't talk to me, you don't talk to Katherine, you can't wait to get out of the house and up your favourite girder. (*Sobbing quietly*) You don't like me any more, I know you don't—I'm boring for you, I haven't got what you want, and you don't want to hear the things I tell you because I've got nothing to tell you, nothing happens . . .

Albert I like a quiet life, that's all.

Kate Gutless. You'll spend your whole life painting that bridge . . .

Albert It's a good job.

Kate You know damn well it's a stupid job which any thick idiot could do—but you're educated, Albert. You had opportunities. There was Metal Alloys and Allied Metals—you could have gone right up the ladder—we'd have a house, and friends, and we'd entertain and Katherine would have nice friends, you could have been an executive!

Albert I was lying in bed one day when the maid came in to make it. She was all starchy, when she moved her skirt sort of crackled against her nylons. I never had any regrets, but I did want her to be happy too.

Kate (*sobbing*) I've begun talking to myself, over the sink and the stove . . . I talk to myself because nobody else listens, and you won't talk to me, so I talk to the sink and the stove and the baby, and maybe one day one of them will answer me.

The baby gurgles, almost managing to say a word

The scene closes

SCENE 16

The bridge.

Albert is discovered painting.

Albert (*crooning flatly amid and around the tune of "Night and Day"*)
Night and day, I am the one . . .
day and night, I'm really a part of me—
I've got me under my skin.
So why
don't I take all of me.
When I begin the beguine—
I depend on the mood I'm in.

I get accustomed to my face,
The thought of me makes me stop
before I begin.
Yes, I've got me under my skin,
and I get a kick out of me.

Day and night, night and day. . . .
Shall I compare me to a summer's day,
'Cos I can't get me out of my mind
I saw me in Monterey . . .
and I'm all right by me,
yes, I'm all right, I'm all right,
I'm all right by me. . . .

Fraser enters on the bridge, applauding

Who's there? Who's that?

Fraser (*applauding*) Very nice, very nice. The egotist school of
songwriting.

Albert Who are you?

Fraser You mean my name?

Albert I suppose so.

Fraser Fraser.

Albert What are you doing on my bridge?

Fraser Yours?

Albert I'm painting it. I'm authorized.

Fraser You've got a big job ahead of you.

Albert I've got the time.

Fraser You've got the time perhaps, but I'd say that time is
against you. The condition of the paintwork is very shoddy.

Albert Well, it hasn't been done for a fair while.

Fraser Yes, it's beginning to look definitely tatty.

Albert I'm getting through it bit by bit.

Fraser Too slow. The old paint isn't lasting. People have noticed,
you know. There's been talk.

Albert Look here—are you the bridge inspector or something?

Fraser What?

Albert Did Mr Fitch send you?

Fraser Who?

Albert What's it all about then?

Fraser Look down there. I came up because up was the only
direction left. The rest has been filled up and is still filling. The
city is a hold in which blind prisoners are packed wall to wall.
Motor cars nose each other down every street, and they are
beginning to breed, spread, they press the people to the walls
by their knees, pinning them by their knees, and there's no end
to it, because if you stopped making them, thousands of people
would be thrown out of work, and they'd have no money to
spend, the shopkeepers would get caught up in it, and the
farms and the factories, and all the people dependent on
them, with their children and all. There's too much of everything, but the space for it is constant. So the shell of human
existence is filling out, expanding, and it's going to bang.

Albert You're frightened of the traffic?

Fraser We are at the mercy of a vast complex of moving parts,
any of which might fail. Civilization is in decline and the white
rhino is being wiped out for the racket in bogus aphrodisiacs.

Albert An animal lover . . .

Fraser That was merely a trifle I snatched at in my inability to
express the whole. I have never been able to understand, for
instance, why anyone should want to be a dentist. I cannot
pin down the divinity which ensures that just so many people
take up dentistry and just so many agree to milk the cows
which would otherwise scream in pain just as children would
scream if there were no dentists.

Albert I see. A lunatic, in fact.

Fraser Not certifiably so. By no means certified. I am simply
open, wide open, to certain insights. I do not believe that there
is anyone in control. There is the semblance of pattern—
supply meeting demand, one-way streets, give and take, the
presumption of return tickets, promises to pay the bearer on
demand, et cetera—but there's nothing really holding it together. One is forced to recognize the arbitrariness of what we
claim to be order. Somewhere there is a lynch pin, which,
when removed, will collapse the whole monkey-puzzle. And
I'm not staying there till it happens.

Albert I see. Well, we all have our problems, but I don't see how
that justifies you climbing about council property. So would
you kindly descend . . .

Fraser That's what I came up here for.

Albert To descend?

Fraser It never occurred to me to stay.

Albert You came up to go down?

Fraser To jump.

Albert Jump?

Fraser Off.

Albert Jump off? You'd kill yourself. Ah.

Fraser Yes.

Albert I see. All right then.

Fraser My mind was made up . . .

Albert I see your point.

Fraser It seemed the easiest thing to to.

Albert I agree. Well then, time is hurrying by, waiting for no man. Or is that tide?

Fraser I see you're trying to humour me. Well, I expected that. You'll be sending for a priest next.

Albert Come, come, don't prevaricate.

Fraser What?

Albert I mean proscrastinate.

Fraser Me?

Albert You said you were going to jump.

Fraser Well?

Albert Well—jump.

Fraser Aren't you going to try to talk me out of it?

Albert You know your own mind. And you're holding me up. I've got to paint where you're standing.

Fraser You wouldn't just stand there without lifting a finger?

Albert I knew it. You're just a talker. Those ones never do it.

Fraser I can't believe it. You wouldn't just stand there and watch me kill myself.

Albert I thought that's what you wanted.

Fraser Well, I did. I couldn't bear the noise, and the chaos. I couldn't get free of it, the enormity of that disorder, so dependent on a chance sequence of action and reaction. So I started to climb, to get some height, you know, enough height to drop from, to be sure, and the higher I climbed, the more I saw and the less I heard. And look now. I've been up here for hours, looking down and all it is, is dots and bricks, giving out a gentle hum. Quite safe. Quite small after all. Quite ordered, seen from above. Laid out in squares, each square a function, each dot a functionary. I really think it might work. Yes, from a vantage point like this, the idea of society is just about tenable.

Albert Funked it. Well, mind how you go. Don't fall.

The scene closes

SCENE 17

The committee-room.

The Chairman, Dave, Fitch and George are in session.

The Chairman Gentlemen. This special emergency meeting of the Clufton Bay Bridge Sub-Committee has been called as a result of public representations, both direct and via the press, concerning the unsightly condition of what is the symbol of Clufton's prosperity. My grandfather who was loved by the public, and owed everything to them, must be turning in his grave. It is a salutary reminder that we are all servants of the public, Mr Fitch.

Dave Hear hear, Mr Chairman.

The Chairman Shut up, Dave. As chairman, I of course take full responsibility. That is the duty of the chairman, regardless of where that responsibility actually lies, Mr Fitch.

George Hear hear, Mr Chairman.

The Chairman It is no smiling matter, George. The City publicity officer has been on to me, the Parks and Amenities have been on to me, British Railways have been on to me, and the *Clufton Chronicle* has been doing its damnedest to get on to me. This committee is the shame and laughing-stock of the Clufton Council, and as the future—as a possible future Mayor, I am gravely embarrassed by having to carry the can for a lack of foresight and watchfulness on the part of committee members whose names I will not mention, George. I have issued a statement to the effect that the squalid state of disrepair of Clufton's highly respected bridge is the result of a miscalculation by a senior public official, for which I as chairman take full responsibility, Mr Fitch.

Fitch (*a broken man*) I can only say in mitigation that I have been under pressure—a sick man—domestic and financial worries . . .

The Chairman Quite, quite. Let's stick to essentials. Two years ago, at your insistence and against my better judgment which I left unspoken in deference to your professional capacity, we arranged to switch to improved paint lasting eight years, and through a reasoning which I never pretended to follow, to sack three of the four painters. Today, two years later, we are left with a bridge that is only one quarter painted while the other three-quarters is in a condition ranging from the sub-standard to the decrepit. Now then—what happened?

Fitch Mr Chairman, gentlemen, I have served Clufton man and boy for five years. Clufton is the repository of my dreams and boyhood memories, the temple of my hopes to transform the running of a living community to a thing of precision and efficiency, a cybernetic poem—a programmed machine as perfect as a rose . . .

The Chairman For God's sake, Fitch, pull yourself together.

Fitch Gentlemen, let us take as our starting point the proposition that X painters painting at the rate of Y would take Z years to paint surface ABC. We found that when X equalled four, Z equalled two, Y and ABC remaining constant. Then along came the factor P, a paint lasting eight years . . .

The Chairman I can't stand it.

George I think what Mr Fitch is getting at, Mr Chairman, is that the brown paint on the bridge was only supposed to last two years, the time that it took four painters to finish the job and start again. Well, of course, when we cut down to one painter using eight-year paint, it was obvious that in two years' time he'd only be a quarter of the way along, so the old paint would be ready for another coat.

The Chairman If it was obvious why didn't you say so?

George I couldn't catch the eye of the chairman. Of course, if we could hang on for another six years, Mr Fitch would emerge triumphantly vindicated as the poet of precision and efficiency.

The Chairman I might be dead in six years.

Dave Hear hear, Mr Chairman.

The Chairman Thank you, Dave. So what are we going to do about it? Fitch?

Fitch Er . . . if we hired extra painters, one to start at the far
end, one in the middle going one way, another going the oppo-
site way, no—er, the progressive element intercedes—if we
have two painters back to back at a point nine-sixteenths from
the far end—no . . .

The Chairman We'd better go back to the old system and hire
three more painters. Carry on from there.

Fitch You can't do that! They wouldn't be quick enough on the
one hand and they'd finish too soon on the other—you see,
the bridge won't need repainting for another six years, and the
resultant coefficient—waste and unsightliness—the entire
system would disintegrate and cost thousands . . .

The Chairman Money? (*Appalled*) My grandfather . . .

George I think I see a way out, Mr Chairman. From the points
of view of efficiency and expediency, I think we can get the
whole thing resolved with just a bit of organization.

Fitch Every day counts.

George One day is all we'll need.

The scene closes

SCENE 18

Albert's home.

Albert and Kate are discovered.

Albert Met a feller up on the bridge the other day.

Kate (*strained*) Oh, yes?

Albert Yes. Climbed up to chuck himself off.

Kate Did he?

Albert No. (*He goes to the door*) Once he got up there, the mood
passed.

Kate Albert . . .

Albert (*going*) Just off.

Kate You used to say good-bye.

The scene closes

SCENE 19

The bridge.

Albert is discovered painting. Fraser enters.

Fraser Hello.
Albert Who's that?
Fraser Me again.
Albert Did you forget something?
Fraser No, it all came back to me. After I went down, it all started again. So I came back up.
Albert To jump?
Fraser Yes.
Albert Go on then.
Fraser I'm all right again now. I don't want to.
Albert Now look here, this isn't a public right of way. I'll report you.
Fraser I can't help it. I'm forced up and coaxed down. I'm a victim of perspective.
Albert (*shouting*) Get down!
Fraser (*moving down*) All right, I'm going.

The scene closes

SCENE 20

Fitch's office.

Albert and Fitch are discovered talking.

Albert I'm not a complaining man. I let people get on with their own lives, I'm sympathetic to problems, but a line must be drawn. I've found him up there four times now, Mr Fitch, and each time it's the same story—he doesn't want to jump after all. I've given him every chance.
Fitch Yes, yes, but that isn't what I've asked to see you about at all. You haven't been listening to me.
Albert It's unnerving me, finding company up there. Well, it's changing the character of the job, and playing hell with my schedule—simply on the level of efficiency I protest.

Fitch Well, as I say, for the reasons given, the matter is to be resolved. We have to get the bridge finished by the end of the week.

Albert What?

Fitch We can't allow further deterioration. The public is roused.

Albert Wait a minute—I can't possibly finish by the end of the week.

Fitch I realize of course you'll need help. I have made arrangements.

Albert What arrangements?

Fitch Eighteen hundred painters will report for work at seven o'clock tomorrow morning. By nightfall the job will be done. I have personally worked it out and my department has taken care of the logistics.

Albert Eighteen hundred?

Fitch Seventeen hundred and ninety-nine. I kept a place for you. I thought you'd like that.

The scene closes

SCENE 21

Albert's home.

Kate is sitting alone. Albert rushes in.

Albert (*breathlessly*) They're moving in on me, the dots are ganging up. I'll need food and spare clothes, a couple of blankets . . .

Kate rises and goes out

What are you doing?

Kate (*off*) Packing, Albert. I'm going.

Albert Kate, they've got it in for me. They're trying to move me off—and I've earned my position. I've worked for it.

Kate enters

Kate I've got a position—a housemaid, living in. With Katherine. I'll let you know my days off, for visiting.

Albert (*after a pause*) Kate—I'm sorry. Will you come and see
    me sometimes? Will you come along and wave?

The scene closes

SCENE 22

The bridge.

Albert is working and singing, more rapidly than before.

Dip brush, dip brush—slap it on, slide silver
over the iron, glide like mercury—slick, wipe,
tickle it wet, swish, slop, sweep and wipe the
silver slime, it's all I can do—
in eight years I'll be pushing thirty-two
a manic painter coming through for the second time.
Dip brush, dip brush . . .

Fraser enters on the bridge

Fraser What's the rush?
Albert Fraser. (*He stops painting*)
Fraser You're going at it.
Albert (*shouting*) Get down! Get down!
Fraser This isn't like you at all.
Albert I'm not having you up here.
Fraser There's room for both of us.
Albert You're just the first, and I'm not going to have it. If
    you're going to jump—jump.
Fraser That's why I came, again.
Albert (*quietly*) You're going to jump?
Fraser No. Not today.
Albert (*furiously*) Up and down like a yo-yo!
Fraser I agree that it is ludicrous. Down there I am assailed by
    the flying splinters of a world breaking up at the speed of
    procreation without end. The centre cannot hold and the out-
    side edge is filling out like a balloon, without the assurance of

infinity. More men are hungry than honest, and more eat than produce. The apocalypse cannot be long delayed——

Albert You'd be better out of it. I'll tell them why you did it, if that's what's worrying you.

Fraser —so I climb up again and prepare to cast myself off, without faith in angels to catch me—or desire that they should—and lo!—I look down at it all and find that the proportions have been re-established. My confidence is restored by perspective.

Albert But it's my bridge . . .

Fraser You think only of yourself—you see yourself as the centre, whereas I know that I am not placed at all . . .

Albert There are other bridges—bigger . . .

Fraser (*listening*) What's that?

Albert San Francisco—Sydney——

Fraser Listen.

Albert —Brooklyn—there's a place for you——

Fraser Listen!

Albert —but I was here first—this is mine . . . (*He tails off*)

There is the faintest sound of eighteen hundred men marching, whistling "Colonel Bogey"

Fraser There's an army on the march . . .

Albert So they're coming . . .

Fraser A solid phalanx moving squarely up the road, an officer at the head . . .

Albert Fitch.

Fraser But they're not soldiers.

Albert He's mad.

Fraser (*appalled*) They're just—people.

Albert (*shouting—to the people*) Go away!

Fraser Coming here.

Albert Halt! About turn!

Fraser They've lined up hundreds and hundreds of ordinary people—the overflow—all the the fit men in the prime of life —they're always the ones on the list—preference is given to the old and the sick, the women and children—when it comes to the point, it's the young and able-bodied who go first . . .

Albert Can't you see—they're taking over!

Fraser Ten abreast—sixty deep—and another phalanx behind— and another—successive waves——

The whistling gets louder

    —so it has come to this.

Albert They're going to come up!

Fraser It was the only direction left.

Albert They're going to wheel right . . .

Fitch (*off, in the distance*) Right—wheel!

Albert Off the road and through the gate . . .

Fitch (*off*) Straighten up there!

Albert Up to the end of the bridge, on to the tracks . . .

Fraser That's it then—they have finally run out of space, the edges have all filled out and now there is only up.

Albert Eighteen hundred men—flung against me by a madman! Was I so important? Here they come.

The tramp-tramp of the march becomes louder, ringing hollow progressively as more and more leave terra firma and reach the bridge

    (*Approaching tears*) I could have done it, given time . . .

Fraser There will be more behind them—the concrete-mixers churn and churn until only a single row of corn grows between two cities, and is finally ground between their walls . . .

Albert They didn't give me a fair chance—I would have worked nights . . .

Fraser They'll all come following—women and children too— and those that are at the top will be pushed off like disgraced legionaires . . .

Albert I had it under control—ahead of schedule . . .

Fraser Ah well. But they should be breaking step.

The tramping increases

    Like soldiers do when they come to a bridge . . .

Albert I was all right—I was doing well . . .

Fraser For the very good reason——

The tramping increases

    —that if they don't——

Albert I was still young—fit——

Fraser —the pressures cannot bounce—but build and have to break out——

The rivets of the bridge start to pop

Albert —good head for heights——
Fraser —they don't know, or don't believe it, but the physical laws are inviolate——

There is a sound of cracking and wrenching

Albert What's happening?
Fraser —and if you carry on like that a bridge will shiver, the girders tensed and trembling for the release of the energy being driven through them——
Albert —it's breaking up!
Fraser —until the rivets pop—
Albert (*screaming*) What are they doing to my bridge!
Fraser —and a forty-foot girder moans like a jew's harp——

A loud Twang! is heard

—and one's enough . . .
Albert To go to such lengths! I didn't do them any harm! What did I have that they wanted?

The bridge collapses, and—

the CURTAIN *falls*

FURNITURE AND PROPERTY LIST

SCENE 1

On stage: 4 sets of painting equipment

SCENES 2, 17

On stage: Large table
4 chairs

SCENE 3

On stage: Small bed
Bedside chair

SCENES 4, 20

On stage: Desk. *On it:* writing materials
Desk chair
Small chair

SCENE 5

On stage: Dining table set for breakfast for three
3 chairs

SCENES 6, 8, 10, 12, 16, 19, 22

On stage: 1 set of painting equipment

SCENES 7, 9

On stage: 2 armchairs
Occasional table

SCENES 11, 13, 18, 21

On stage: As Scene 7, but add baby, cot, and rattle

SCENE 15

On stage: As Scene 11, but add 2 cups and saucers on table

LIGHTING PLOT

Property fittings required: nil
Various internal and external settings

EFFECTS PLOT

SCENE 1

SCENE 14

SCENE 22